Travelling About

By Sally Hewitt
Photographs by Chris Fairclough

W
FRANKLIN WATTS
LONDON • SYDNEY

This edition 2003

Franklin Watts
96 Leonard Street
London EC2A 4XD

Franklin Watts Australia
45-51 Huntley Street
Alexandria
NSW 2015

Editor: Samantha Armstrong
Designer: Louise Snowdon
Consultant: Steve Watts, School of Education, University of Sunderland

A CIP catalogue record for this book is
available from the British Library
Dewey Decimal Classification Number: 388.4

ISBN 0 7496 5201 2

Printed in Malaysia

Contents

On your bike

Bicycles have two wheels and no engine. A cyclist works hard to travel about. You can ride a bicycle to keep fit or just for fun.

• If you needed to get somewhere quickly, would you walk or cycle?

A helmet protects a cyclist's head.

• How else can a cyclist keep safe?

Some journeys are too long to cycle easily.

• What other things would make you choose not to cycle?

The sign tells pedestrians and cyclists which side of the white line on the pavement to use.

• Why are pedestrians and cyclists kept apart?

Going in the car

Many families have a car and some have two.
These boys travel to school in the family car.

- Do you travel to school in a car? What other ways are there to get to school?
- Are the roads busy when you travel to school?

There is room in the car boot for everything the boys need to take with them to school.

- What other things could be carried in the boot?
- How do you carry your things to school?

The driver and the passengers must put on their safety belts before they set off.

- Why is it important to use a safety belt?

Filling up with fuel

All vehicles with an engine need fuel to go.
Drivers stop at a petrol station to fill up their tanks.

- What can you see around this petrol station?
- Why has it been built here?

A tanker delivers fuel to the petrol station.

- Why is the tanker so big?
- When the fuel is delivered to the station, where do you think it is stored?

Fuel is not the only thing on sale here.

- What else can you buy?
- Why is the price of fuel written in big numbers?

11

Roadworks!

Roadworks blocking the road can cause a traffic jam.
Roadworkers try to keep the traffic moving along.

- What part of the road has been blocked off?
- How do the drivers know when to stop or go?

Signs let drivers know what is happening. Other signs give instructions to drivers.

• Where are the best places to put these signs?

Cones show drivers where they are not allowed to go.

• Are the signs and cones easy to move? Why?

13

On the motorway

On a motorway traffic travels quickly for long distances without stopping.

• What different vehicles are using this motorway?
• Imagine how many vehicles pass this spot every day.

There are three lanes in each direction, an exit lane and a hard shoulder at the edge. The exit lane is for vehicles that are getting off the motorway. A barrier in the centre separates the traffic going in opposite directions.

• Vehicles are not supposed to stop on the hard shoulder except in an emergency. Can you think why?
• Would you like to live near a motorway?

Catching a bus

A bus can carry a lot of people on a journey.
Passengers get on and off at bus stops along the way.

- How is travelling on a bus different from travelling in a car?
- How is it the same?

Information

Your local bus map

A timetable tells you what time the bus leaves and when it should arrive at the stop where you want to get off.

- What kind of journeys would you choose to make by bus?

Thornton Heath Pond
Norbury Streatham
Streatham Hill Brixton Hill 109

BRIXTON STATION

Bus number 109 is going to Brixton Station.

- Why do you think each bus has a number?

Traffic moves slowly along a busy road.

- How does a bus lane help a bus to arrive on time?

Trams

A tram travels on tracks through some towns and cities, carrying passengers from stop to stop.

- How is a tram the same as a bus?
- How is a tram the same as a train?

Wherever you see metal tracks in the road, look out for trams.

Electricity from overhead cables powers the tram on its way.

• What kind of fuel do buses, cars and trucks use?
• Why is electricity a good way to power trams?

People buy their tram tickets from a machine before they get on board.

• What other journeys do you need a ticket for?

Special journeys

Every day vehicles make special journeys. In parts of Scotland, a postbus delivers mail to homes far away from towns and villages. People can ride in the postbus to go shopping or to see friends.

• Why do you think it is called a postbus?
• Would you like to use the postbus to go shopping?

Emergency vehicles such as fire engines and ambulances make life-saving journeys. Other traffic moves aside so they can get through quickly.

• How do emergency vehicles warn traffic that they are there?

Paramedics load a stretcher onto the ambulance.

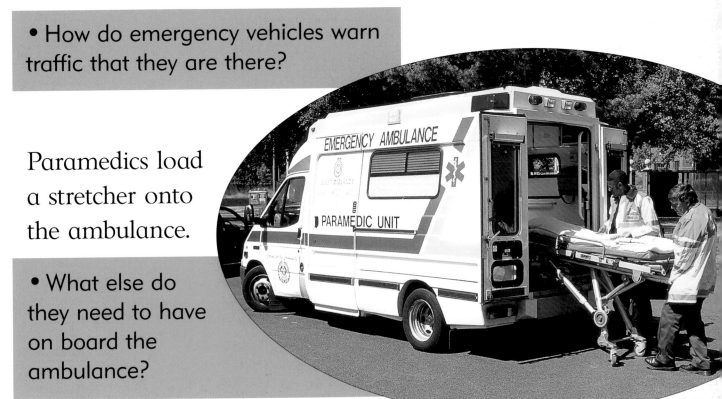

• What else do they need to have on board the ambulance?

Taking the train

A train travels quickly along railway tracks across the country from station to station. The driver sits in a cab at the front.

- How is travelling along tracks different from driving along a road?
- What kind of journey might you make by train?

Sacks of letters and parcels are loaded onto the train.

- What else could a train carry?

Passengers get on and off the train at this busy station. Some people ride bicycles to the station. They leave them there until they return.

• Why do you think some people cycle to the station?
• What sounds would you hear at the station?
• What can passengers do on a train journey?

Level crossing

The place where a railway crosses a road is called a level crossing. When a train approaches, barriers come down to keep people and traffic off the railway line.

• What else can you see in the picture that makes the crossing safe?
• What other ways could a railway cross a road?

Red lights flash to warn pedestrians and traffic that a train is coming.

• Why do you think vehicles are not allowed to stop in the yellow box marked on the road?

The train passes by and the barriers go up to let people and traffic over the crossing.

25

Travelling by boat

Sometimes we need to cross over water when travelling about.

• What different ways are there to cross water?

A ferry carries cars, trucks and coaches as well as passengers across the water.

Vehicles drive up a ramp onto the ferry. The ramp is at the back, or stern, of the ferry.

• What happens to the ramp when the ferry sets sail?

The ferry sets off across the water.

- Can you see the loading doors at each end of the ferry?
- Why are there doors at both ends?

The drivers park their cars and go to sit in the passenger lounge for the journey. Sometimes the sea is rough.

- Would you like to travel on a ferry?
- Why?

Key words

Barriers   barriers stop people and vehicles from going into a place or area, often for their safety.

Cab   a cab is the front of the train where the driver sits.

Cable   electricity flows through bundles of wires called cables. A tram is powered by electricity from overhead cables.

Car boot   a boot is a space, usually at the back of a car, for putting shopping or luggage.

Countryside   the countryside is outside towns and cities. Fields, woods and hills are part of the countryside.

Emergency   an emergency is a dangerous situation that must be seen to as quickly as possible. A fire or a road accident are emergencies.

Fuel   cars, trucks and buses need to burn fuel to give them the energy to move. Petrol is a kind of fuel.

Hard shoulder   a hard shoulder is a motorway lane which is kept clear. Traffic is only allowed to go there in an emergency.

Journey   when you go from one place to another. You might go by bicycle, car, train or even by aeroplane.

Paramedic   paramedics help doctors to look after patients. They drive ambulances and are usually the first to arrive in an emergency.

Pedestrians   people who are walking, not driving or riding a bicycle.

Ramp   a ramp is a slope. Anything with wheels can go up or down it easily.

Traffic jam   a queue of traffic that is moving slowly or has stopped.

Vehicle   something that carries people or things from place to place. A bicycle, car and bus are all kinds of vehicles.

Think about travel

1. Think of a place you would like to go.
   - How could you get there?
   - What would you see on your journey?

2. Think about travelling by train.
   - What would you need to know to plan your trip?
   - What jobs do people do at the station or on the train?

3. Look at a map of where you live.
   - Find the roads, railway lines and the street where you live.
   - Find other places you know, such as your school, on the map. Follow with your finger the roads that you would take to get from one place to another.

4. Keep a record of all the journeys you make in one week, even the short ones.
   - Why did you make each journey?
   - Did you walk or go by car? How did you get there?
   - Did you enjoy the journey?

5. Find somewhere safe to watch traffic on a busy road.
   - Make a note of the different kinds of vehicles you see.
   - What kind of journey do you think they are making?

Index